AMERICAN ENGLISH PUNCTUATION FOR ANYONE

A Friendly Reference

George Ann Gregory, Ph.D.

Tanya Bibeau, Editor

Published by MTG Publishing, 7012 Petit Ave, Van Nuys, CA 91406

Manufactured in the United States of America.

ISBN 0-9704060-1-0

About the Author

George Ann Gregory has a Ph.D. in Applied Linguistics. She is a lifelong educator who has developed language and literacy with ages preschool through adults.

She has worked with a variety of ethnic and linguistic groups, including Amerindian, Southeast Asian, Latin American, Middle-Eastern, European, African American, Hispanic American, and Anglo American.

Her research includes grammatical analysis of compositions and teaching methods that work. Her publications include research articles, essays, short stories, poetry, and children's stories and texts.

OTHER PUBLISHED WORKS

BY

GEORGE ANN GREGORY

A Basic Grammar Dictionary for Anyone
A Grammar Dictionary written for high school and college students, English Language Learners, teachers, business people, writers, and editors.

Grammar Works for Better Writing
Series Developer and Coordinator
A series of grammar workbooks and teacher manuals for students in grades 3 through 9.

TABLE OF CONTENTS

SECTION I: PUNCTUATION RULES

TABLE OF CONTENTS

(CONTINUED)

INTRODUCTION

WHY PUNCTUATE?

When you write, the person(s) you are communicating to cannot see your facial expressions or hear the tone of your voice to get the full meaning. Punctuation helps a reader understand your full meaning. In American English, there are a set of rules to help you. This book contains those rules.

The advent of computers and word processing has made the use of punctuation marks such as the en and em dashes, ellipses and bullets more accessible. This book will give you the rules for their usage.

STYLISTIC CONVENTIONS

Although closely related, punctuation and style play different roles. Where punctuation helps your reader to understand how you are communicating, style shows your reader a certain pattern or flow to your writing. There are many different styles used in modern writing.

The Stylistic Conventions section contains suggestions for formal writing conventions and written samples, including a friendly letter, business letter, résumé, essay, and excerpts from research papers.

THE APPENDIX

The Appendix contains lists and charts of abbreviations, contractions, hyphenated words, and transition words for sentences and paragraphs. As a note, it is always a good idea to check a dictionary to determine the correct hyphenation of a word or words.

GRAMMAR AND PUNCTUATION

Certain grammatical structures require certain punctuation. Thus, a good understanding of punctuation can be more easily attained if one has a good understanding of grammar or learns both disciplines simultaneously.

SECTION I

PUNCTUATION RULES

Punctuation: The use of periods, commas, and other marks to help make the meaning of written works clear. Punctuation does for writing what pauses and changes of voice do for speech.

Etymology: From Medieval Latin and Latin roots. Its original meaning suggests "to point."

THE APOSTROPHE

,

Apostrophe: A punctuation mark used to show possession or omissions in spelling.

Etymology: From Latin and Greek roots. Its original meaning suggests "turning away from."

APOSTROPHE

I *can't* find the pickles.

English uses an apostrophe to show that a letter or letters have been left out of certain types of words.

Grandpa *John's* mule is in the pasture.

Apostrophes are used in contractions or nouns that show ownership.

CONTRACTIONS

She *didn't* come to dinner.

He's owned five cars in the past year.

They'll be here shortly.

It is almost five *o'clock*.

Use an apostrophe in contractions. You make a contraction when you put two or more words together to make one.

"Go get 'em!" she yelled excitedly.

You make a contraction when you shorten a single word, which is often done in dialogue. **See the Contractions Chart in the Appendix.**

OWNERSHIP: SINGULAR OR PLURAL NOUNS

We went to Mrs. *Smith's* house.

Is that *John's* wallet on the desk?

We went to see *Juan's* band last night.

Use an apostrophe with a noun to show ownership or possession. Originally, English used a vowel plus the "s" to show possession. Now the apostrophe takes the place of the vowel.

There goes *Francis'* car

Carlos' band plays downtown tonight.

The *dogs'* leashes were lost.

The *ox's* tail is hurt.

If the singular or plural form of a noun ends in *s* or *x*, add an apostrophe. With single-syllable words that end in *x.*, add an apostrophe and an *s*.

The *child's* hair is brown

The *children's* party is on Saturday.

The *oxen's* yoke shattered.

For singular or plural nouns that do not end in *s* or *x*, add an apostrophe and an *s*.

OWNERSHIP: COMPOUND OR HYPHENATED WORDS

My *father-in-law's* house burned down.

The *cowgirl's* horse neighed softly.

In compound or hyphenated words, add the apostrophe or apostrophe plus "s" at the end of the word. **See also *hyphen.***

OWNERSHIP: COMPOUND SUBJECTS

Laurie and *Carol's* apartment has two bathrooms.

Ed and *Carlos'* class meets every Friday.

When two or more people own something, add the apostrophe or apostrophe plus *s* to the last person's name.

OWNERSHIP: LIVING THINGS

The *cat's* fur was gray and white.

The *plant's* leaves are green and healthy.

Use an apostrophe or apostrophe plus *s* to show ownership of living things.

OWNERSHIP: NON-LIVING THINGS

Correct

The top of the table needs dusting.

Incorrect

The *table's* top needs dusting.

Do not use an apostrophe to show ownership of objects.

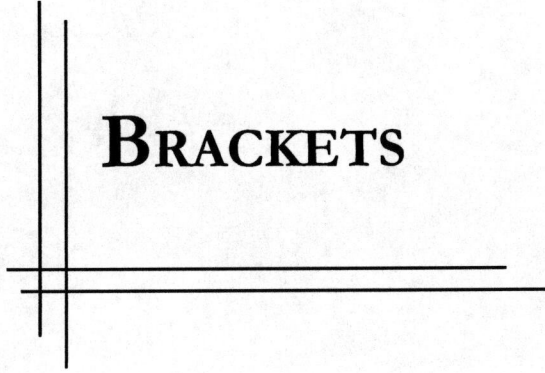

BRACKETS

[ ]

Brackets: A punctuation mark used to enclose words or numerals.

Etymology: From Middle French, Germanic and Latin roots. Its original meaning suggests "breeches."

CLARIFYING A DETAIL

"When we get to Auntie Em's [in Kansas], I'll fix your bicycle," Dad said.

"This group [Checkerspots] consists of small, attractive butterflies."

Use brackets when you need to make clear some detail in another's speech or writing.

CLARIFYING SPELLING IN A QUOTE

"There will be no sterms [storms] that day," the *Almanac* stated.

Use brackets when you need to correct the spelling in a quotation. Only use brackets when you are quoting someone else. **See also *Quotations.***

THE BULLET

●

Bullet: A punctuation mark used at the beginning of each item in a list.

Etymology: From Middle French roots. Its original meaning suggests "ball."

ADVERTISING

- Easy to read
- Affordable
- Available in your local bookstore

Use bullets to highlight items in a list in a brochure, flier, pamphlet, proposal, or newsletter. Bullets call the reader's attention to each item.

LISTS

You will need to bring your own camping equipment.

- Tent
- Camp stove
- Sleeping bag
- Cooking utensils

Be certain to use a period and not a colon at the end of the sentence introducing the list. **See also *Colon* and *Period.***

CAPITALIZATION

CAPITAL

Capital Letters: The large letters of the alphabet.

Etymology: From Latin roots. Its original meaning suggests "of first rank."

SENTENCES

The wind blew the tree down.

He said, "The wind blew the tree down."

"Guinea pigs make cute pets," the salesperson told us.

Use a capital letter to begin the first word in a sentence even when it is inside quotation marks.

PROPER NOUNS

Last year we went to *Cancún*.

Singapore is an exciting city.

She lives on *Park Avenue*.

The new mayor is *Christine Ramirez*.

Mrs. Tyrrell recently retired.

My day off is *Wednesday*.

His birthday is *February* 13th.

Independence Day is her favorite holiday.

Many *Europeans* settled in *America*.

Use a capital letter to begin a proper noun.

Names of Relatives

Pass the peas to *Mom*, please.

I think *Cousin Tom* will be late.

Use a capital letter to begin the name of a relative when you use it for a name and without a possessive pronoun like *his, h*er, or *my*.

Titles

Gone with the Wind is a book about the war between the states.

Isn't that the *William Tell Overture?*

Use capital letters to begin words in a title. Always capitalize the first and last word. You do not capitalize prepositions, conjunctions, and articles. **See also *Italics.***

The Pronoun *I*

Now *I* am ready to go.

I want a pony for Christmas.

Always capitalize the pronoun *I* even when it is part of the contractions *I'm* and *I'll.*

SALUTATIONS AND COMPLIMENTARY CLOSES IN LETTERS

Dear Mom,

Dear Mr. Garcia:

Begin the salutation of a letter with a capital letter. A salutation is the part usually beginning with *Dear.*

Sincerely yours,

Truly yours,

Begin the complimentary close of a letter with a capital letter. A complimentary close is the part that usually begins with *Sincerely, Yours truly, Truly yours,* etc.

OUTLINES

   I. Introduction
      A. History of problem

      B. Summary of problem

      C. Proposed solution to problem

Use a capital letter to begin the first word in each heading and subheading of an outline.

COLONS

It was an outstanding movie: It had a surprise ending.

Use a capital letter to begin the first word in a sentence following a colon. **See also Colon.**

THE INTERJECTION *O*

Rejoice , *O* people, rejoice.

Capitalize the interjection *O*.

PERSONIFIED NOUNS

Goodness overcomes *Evil.*

Here the noun *evil* takes on an almost human quality. This is called a personified noun. Capitalizing it tells the reader how you are using the word.

EXCLAMATIONS

Hurry up!   She said, "Hurry up!"

Hey!   "Hey!" he shouted.

Use a capital letter to begin exclamations that act like a sentence even when it is a quotation.

THE COLON

:

Colon: A punctuation mark most commonly used before a series of items, explanations or long quotations. A colon has other uses as well.

Etymology: From Greek and Latin roots. Its original meaning suggests "member of a body or sentence."

LISTS

Donna had four dishes with chile: salsa, green chile stew, red chile posole, and green chile and corn.

We need the following items for the party: hats, candles, plates, napkins, and forks.

Use a colon to introduce a list at the end of a sentence.

COMMON ERRORS WITH LISTS

Have the students find words that rhyme with red, *such as:* head, bed, and Ted.

Do not use a colon after *such as.*

Many people came to the party, *including:* the Smiths, the Jones, and the Browns.

Do not use a colon after *including.*

The following people will *go:*
Lisa Whitt
Rita Pollack

Do not use a colon after a verb.

EXPLANATIONS

Democracy is truly an American idea: Native Americans had been practicing it for centuries before the Europeans came.

The child was remarkably imaginative: She created an entire city in the living room filled with fairies, princes, and princesses by using story books, figurines, and coffee tables.

Use a colon between sentences when the second sentence explains the first. Remember to capitalize the second sentence.

He showed her a good time: a movie with popcorn.

There are several ways to get to New York: by train, by bus, or by plane for example.

Use a colon to introduce an example or explanation of something you just mentioned.

QUOTATIONS

Mr. Thomas gives us the following definition for *kinesiology:* "Kinesiology is the study of movement—human movement to be specific. I like to think of it as applied physiology."

In a recent book review by Maxine Eggensperger says this: "The book covers the entire century from birth during the early part of the century through WWII to retirement."

In an essay, when you introduce a quotation of more than one line, use a colon. Notice that the colon does not follow the verb but comes after a pronoun or noun.

The Governor claimed, "There will be a twenty percent tax reduction": He did not say when the reduction would go into effect.

When you use a colon at the end of the quote put it outside of the quotation marks.

SALUTATIONS IN BUSINESS LETTERS

Dear Mayor Sanchez:

To Whom it May Concern:

Dear Dr. Nguyen:

Use a colon after the salutation in a formal letter. A salutation is the part usually beginning with *Dear*.

TIME

10:15   1:23   5:42

Use a colon between the hour and the minutes when writing the time in numerals.

THE COMMA

,

Comma: A punctuation mark used to separate structures in a sentence.

Etymology: From Greek and Latin roots. Its original meaning suggests "a piece cut off."

ADJECTIVE CLAUSES

We ate with my oldest brother Donald, *who had just returned from Saudi Arabia.*

Ashley and Luis came to our dance practice, *which we hadn't yet started.*

Yesterday I saw Sihn Chang, *who is our best soccer player.*

Use a comma before an adjective clause when it does not give defining information. This is called a nonrestrictive or non-defining clause. In the above examples, the adjective clause provides additional information. Without the adjective clause, you can still understand the sentence.

James Smiley, *who published his first poem at age seven,* is a citizen of the Dine (Navajo) Nation.

This book, *which was published last year,* has become a primary text in business.

The use of atomic energy is possible due in part to the theories of Albert Einstein, *whose perspective on life was unique.*

Use a pair of commas, one before and one after, with a non-defining clause when it comes somewhere else in the sentence other than the end.

CONJUNCTIONS

Uncle Pat called the boys for dinner, *and* they came running.

Use a comma before a conjunction *(and, but, or, nor, for, so, yet)* when you join two main or independent clauses. If you use a comma, you must also have a conjunction.

They were small *but* feisty.

You do not need a comma before a conjunction joining only two words or phrases.

Mrs. Wright worked us hard in her English class. *But* she was a very fair teacher.

You do not use a comma after a conjunction even if it begins a sentence.

INTRODUCTORY CLAUSES

Since we are friends, I want you to come to my birthday party.

When we finish work, we will go to dinner.

Because everyone was still asleep, she tiptoed quietly through the house.

Use a comma after an introductory clause.

INTRODUCTORY PHRASES

During the morning, the squirrels ate all the birdseed.

Running hard, the girls finally caught up with the boys.

Use a comma after an introductory phrase.

INTRODUCTORY WORDS

Lazily, the river sings us a lullaby.

However, we still want our raises.

Happily, the child skipped down the lane.

Use a comma after an introductory word.

Now is a good time to stop.

Tomorrow we will go fishing.

You do not need to add a comma after an introductory word or phrase if the meaning is clear without it.

We still, *however,* want our raises.

In this case, a conjunctive adverb has been inserted into the sentence. You need two commas, one before and one after.

ITEMS IN A SERIES

Juanita, Tran, and *Billy* are the best soccer players in the school.

The horse *neighed, raised her head,* and *bucked suddenly.*

Our instructor asked each of us *what our names were, what our major was,* and *why we were taking the class.*

Each person was asked to bring one of the following items: *bananas, apples, oranges,* or *pears.*

Use a comma between three or more words, phrases, and clauses in a series. The words in a series must all be of the same type: for example, nouns with nouns, adjectives with adjectives, predicates with predicates, and clauses with clauses. You must put a comma before the *and.*

She wore a blue hat and a red dress.

The horse neighed and nuzzled my neck.

The police officer asked us who we were and where we were going.

When there are only two items in the series, you do not use a comma.

DATES

My grandmother was born September 3, 1899, in Mississippi.

I sent the letter on March 2, 1947.

Use commas after the day and the year of a date unless it comes at the end of the sentence.

ADDRESSES

I live at 400 North Gabriel Avenue, Santa Domingo, New Mexico.

We arrived at 505 Fifth Avenue, New York City, New York, to visit my aunt.

Use a comma to separate parts of an address.

NUMERALS

The Choctaw ceded 10,423,130 acres of land to the United States government in the year 1830.

Use commas to mark groups of three digits in large numbers. Begin comma separation by counting the digits from right to left. Do not use a comma in a group of numbers representing a year.

NAMES IN REVERSE ORDER

Nguyen, Michael

Stanciwicz, Betty

Zamora, Araceli

Use a comma after the last name when the last or family name comes before the given name.

SALUTATIONS IN A FRIENDLY LETTER

Dear Mom,

Dear Samuel,

Dear Aunt Shirley,

Use a comma after the salutation or greeting in a friendly letter.

ADDRESSING A PERSON

Bob, can you come over here?

OK, Maude, I'll be right there!

Use commas before and after the name of someone addressed directly. When the name comes at the end or beginning of a sentence, only use one comma.

COMMAS TO PREVENT MISREADING

To the right walls of granite rose several hundred feet above us.

This sentence would be difficult to understand without a comma.

To the right, walls of granite rose several hundred feet above us.

You can use a comma when you need to prevent a misreading of your sentence.

QUOTATIONS:

I have observed that "a penny saved is a penny earned."

When you use a quote after *that,* you do not use a comma.

QUOTATIONS: DIALOGUE

Mom said, "Eat all your peas!"

Use a comma to introduce quoted speech.

"Yuck, I hate peas," I replied.

Use a comma to mark the end of quoted speech when it is followed by who said it. *Who said it* is called the *identifying tag*. The comma goes inside the quotation marks.

"What's that?" asked Juliana.

"Look out!" the lifeguard yelled.

Do not use the comma if the quoted speech ends in a question mark or exclamation point. The identifying tag does not begin with a capital letter.

"I have noticed," the teacher commented, "that students seem to become ill when we have a test."

Here the identifying tag interrupts the quotation. Use a comma at the end of the first break in the quoted speech. Also use a comma at the end of the identifying tag. There is no capital letter when the quoted speech begins again because it is not the beginning of the sentence.

PARTS OF A SENTENCE

Incorrect

Students with no previous training, *were sent to help the customers.*

This sentence has a comma between the subject and the predicate. This is incorrect.

Correct

The students with no previous training were sent to help the survivors.

You do not use a comma to separate the subject from the predicate.

Incorrect

She did not understand, *what we wanted.*

Correct

She did not understand *what we wanted.*

You generally do not use a comma before a subordinate clause coming at the end of the sentence.

CLAUSES, WORDS, AND PHRASES THAT DON'T NEED A COMMA

All poems *postmarked by June 1* will be entered into the contest.

A woman *carrying a gold purse* just walked through the lobby.

Matthew's birthday is in September *not October*.

Please stay inside *until we get back*.

Many runners want to redo the marathon *but only in warm weather*.

The brochure *says the company* is very reliable.

The moans came from soldiers *wounded in battle*.

The child cried pitifully *as she looked at her broken doll*.

All the words, phrases, and clauses in these sentences are essential for the meaning of the sentence. They do not need any commas.

Clauses that Don't Need a Comma

The girl *who spoke to you* is singing today.

I want the quilt *that has a blue star on it.*

I am going someplace *where it is quiet.*

In the above examples, you do not need any commas because each clause gives needed or essential information.

THE DASH

– **En Dash**

— **Em Dash**

Dash: A punctuation mark used in writing to show interruptions, appositives, or omitted words.

Etymology: From Middle English roots. Its original meaning suggests "slap."

EN DASH – AND EM DASH —

There are two types of dashes: The en dash is shorter while the em dash is longer.

EN DASH: IN PLACE OF *To*

> Sherwood worked for the city during the years 1976–1987.
>
> That information is on pages 34–45.
>
> I make the Denver–El Paso run five days a week.

Use the en dash in place of *to* between numbers and destinations.

EM DASH: WORDS, PHRASES, OR CLAUSES THAT SUMMARIZE

> The dancers represented children, youth, adults, and seniors—all ages.
>
> We had curries from India, curries from Burma, and curries from Thailand—all colors and kinds of curries.

Use an em dash when you introduce a word, phrase, or clause that summarizes the words coming before it.

EM DASH: SERIES OF ITEMS USED AS AN APPOSITIVE

> I want you to read books written by foreign authors—British, Mexican, or Chinese.

> Three of the runners—Pat, Frank, and Maurice—were new to the school this year.

Use an em dash before a series of items used as an appositive. When the series interrupts the sentence, use an em dash before and after the series.

EM DASH: INTERRUPTIONS

> All the children were dressed in old clothes—just as anyone could expect in this part of the world—but gave us beaming smiles.

Use an em dash when you have an interruption that adds to the meaning of the sentence but is not grammatically part of the sentence.

> If Governor Jones wants to be re-elected—how did he ever get elected anyway? —He will have to change his policy about taxes.

If the interruption includes a question mark or exclamation point, put those before the em dash.

EM DASH: DIALOGUE

"It was—" he gasped with his last breath.

"Help, I'm—" she shouted as she fell.

Use an em dash in dialogue to show an unfinished statement.

Notes on the Use or Creation of em dashes and en dashes:

Check your word processing program for instructions on how to create en dashes and em dashes.

Try to avoid using too many dashes in your writing because they can become distracting to the reader.

THE
ELLIPSIS

. . .

Ellipsis: A punctuation mark used to show an omission or hesitation in writing.

Etymology: From Greek and Latin roots. Its original meaning suggests "leave out."

OMITTED WORD OR WORDS

> On Sunday, October 13, 1492, Columbus wrote
> in his diary, "As soon as it dawned, many . . .
> people came to the beach . . . very handsome
> people with hair not curly but straight and course
> like horsehair; all of them wide in the forehead
> and head, more so than any other race that I
> have ever seen."

Use the ellipsis (three evenly-spaced dots) when you omit a
word or words in quotes. What you leave out must not be
essential to the basic meaning. **See also *Quotations*.**

AT THE END OF QUOTES

> Columbus wrote, "I should like to leave today for
> the island of Cuba . . .."

> Anna gazed into the ocean, "I wish the haze
> would clear . . .."

Use the ellipsis followed by the correct end punctuation when
you omit the end of a quoted sentence or when you leave one or
more sentences out. Generally, you can only leave off the end
of a quote when it still makes a complete sentence.
See also *Quotations*.

DIALOGUE

"She . . . is still in the house," the frightened boy gasped.

"I'm . . . sorry," she said, the hesitation obvious in her voice and manner.

Use the ellipsis when you show hesitation or halting speech. **See also *Quotations.***

POETRY

I gazed admiringly into that face

. . . .

and sang her a love song

g. anna sanchez

Use a line of ellipses dots when you omit a line of poetry.

Notes:

Check your word processing program for information on how to create ellipses dots.

THE
EXCLAMATION
POINT

!

Exclamation Point: A punctuation mark used to show strong emotions.

Etymology: From Middle French and Latin roots. Its original meaning suggests "to cry out."

WORDS

Hey!

Ouch! That hurt.

Wow! That was an exciting movie.

Use an exclamation point to mark the end of an exclamatory word.

PHRASES

Come in!

Stop that!

What a beautiful dress!

Use an exclamation point to mark the end of an exclamatory phrase.

SENTENCES

We just landed on Mars!

She just won the race!

Don't ever talk to me like that again!

Use the exclamation point to mark the end of an exclamatory sentence.

DIALOGUE

"Don't ever talk to me like that again!" Sara yelled.

John glared angrily, wondering what he had ever seen in the spiteful woman. He turned on his heel and spat, "Then grow up!"

When using exclamation points with dialogue, the exclamation point goes inside the quotation marks. **See also _Quotations._**

Compare

"Hey! Get out of that garbage can!" the old man yelled at the raccoon. He ran toward her, tripped over a rock and fell on his bum! The raccoon saw the howling man on the pavement and ran for her life!

"Hey! Get out of that garbage can!" the old man yelled at the raccoon. He ran toward her, tripped over a rock and fell on his bum. The raccoon saw the howling man on the pavement and ran for her life.

Use exclamation marks sparingly in writing. Too many make a piece of writing less interesting, and the purpose of the mark loses its meaning.

THE
HYPHEN

-

The Hyphen: A punctuation mark used to connect compound words or words with prefixes. Also it is used to break words apart. The hyphen is smaller than the en dash.

Etymology: From Middle French and Latin roots. Its original meaning suggests "in one."

Adjectives

Sally is a six-year-old girl with black hair and brown eyes.

They grew up in a two-room cabin in the middle of a cornfield.

Use a hyphen between adjectives when they form one idea.

When to Use a Hyphen with Adjectives

There are two common ways to determine if you need a hyphen.

Montana has a *big blue* sky.

Montana has a *big and blue* sky.

If you can put *and* between the two adjectives, you do not need a hyphen.

Montana has a blue sky.

Montana has a big sky.

If you can use just one of the words to describe the noun, you do not need a hyphen.

Adjectives in a Series

Would all the *first-*, *second-*, and *third-*grade students come to the gymnasium?

We will be showing the *buff-*, *red-*, and *chocolate-*colored cocker spaniels in the next group?

Use a hyphen after each item in a series of adjectives when the last item requires a hyphen.

Generations

Grandpa John was my *great-grandfather*, and he was your *great-great-grandfather*.

Use a hyphen after *great* when describing generations or relationships.

Compound Words

My *mother-in-law* makes great cakes.

None of the *attorneys-at-law* could free her son from the charge.

Use a hyphen to connect many compound words using a preposition. In plural use, only the noun becomes plural. **See Common Hyphenated Words in the Appendix.**

PREFIXES

Mary is my *co-worker.*

She is one of the *co-owners.*

Use a hyphen after a prefix when the prefix ends in the same letter as the word or when the word begins with *w* or *y.*

Honey, can you *re-nail* this doorframe?

Please *re-edit* your paper on exotic fish, and pay particular attention to your punctuation.

Use a hyphen after the prefix *re* when it means *again.*

We are studying *pre-Revolutionary* American history.

Use a hyphen after any prefix that comes before a proper noun or adjective.

Notes on Prefixes:

Sometimes prefixes such as ante, after, pro, pre, super, ultra, non, *and* well *will not require a hyphen. Check a dictionary to determine when to hyphenate these prefixes.*

Words at the End of a Line

I spent ten minutes listening to an un-
intelligible speech.

My teacher listened admiringly to my correct answer.

You may use a hyphen to break words at the end of a line. Use a dictionary to determine the best place to divide a word. Some forms of writing do not encourage dividing words at the end of a line.

Check a dictionary for the correct spelling of any words with hyphens.

Written Numbers

Thirty-six friends came to my birthday party.

There are only twenty-two ways to use this new pocketknife.

I earned five hundred sixty-six free minutes of long distance from my phone company when three of my friends joined too.

Use a hyphen in compound numbers between 21 to 99 when you write them as words.

ITALICS

Italics

Italics: Letters that slant to the right. Used for certain titles and emphasis of words, etc.

Etymology: Named after an Italian printer from Venice who introduced the style.

TITLES

My favorite book is *Gone with the Wind.*

Sesame Street introduced millions of children to reading.

On Saturday, we went to see *Abbot and Costello Meet the Mummy.*

Use Italics for any major literary work, including television programs, movies, plays, symphonies, operas, books, magazines, newspapers, periodicals, albums, and compact discs. Generally, you use quotation marks to indicate smaller pieces contained within a major work, such as a magazine article, single poem, short story, fable, or essay from a published collection.

TERMS

Grammar is "the study of how words make sentences."

A personal fitness trainer must understand *kinesiology.*

Use Italics the first time you introduce a term in a piece of writing. After that, do not put the word in Italics.

PARENTHESES

( )

Parentheses: Punctuation marks used to enclose a word, phrase, or sentence to explain something within a sentence.

Etymology: From Greek and Latin roots. Its original meaning suggests "to put in beside."

COMMENTS OR CLARIFICATION

Sam wrote a moving song about apartheid. (He has never visited South Africa.) He was able to draw parallels between apartheid and the plight of Native Americans.

Use parentheses to enclose word, phrases, or sentences that you are using to add comments or clarification.

CLARIFICATION OF NUMBERS

The City Council allotted one million, twenty thousand dollars ($1,020,000) for renovation of the reptile house.

Use parentheses to enclose numerals to make spelled out numbers more clear.

PLACEMENT OF THE PERIOD

Yesterday, we saw Romeo and Juliet (a contemporary version by the students in Drama 101).

Using parentheses does not change any other punctuation. Here the period still comes at the end of the sentence. **See also** *Period.*

WITHIN A SENTENCE

> We visited the City Council meeting (the Council members seemed more interested in impressing each other) to see how local government works.

When you have a sentence within parentheses breaking up another sentence, you do not need to capitalize the first word. Since parentheses break up the flow, you want to use them sparingly.

LISTS

> I can give you three reasons for getting enough sleep: (1) cells repair faster when you have enough sleep, (2) you are more mentally alert, and (3) you feel better.

Use parentheses to enclose numerals or letters introducing items in a list.

CITATIONS IN A RESEARCH PAPER

The best way to begin any study is to define the terms. *Kinesiology* means the study of human movement or applied anatomy (Moore, 1999).

You may cite a source for data in a research paper within parentheses.

For more examples, **see the Stylistic Conventions in the Appendix.**

COMMON ERRORS

Incorrect

The students will be coming from many countries, (India, Arabia, Mexico, New Zealand and France) to attend the opening ceremonies.

Do not put a comma before the opening parenthesis.

Correct

The students will be coming from many countries (India, Arabia, Mexico, New Zealand and France) to attend the opening ceremonies.

No comma is needed before the opening parenthesis.

THE
PERIOD

.

The Period: A punctuation mark used to show the end of a sentence or shortened word.

Etymology: From Greek and Latin roots. Its original meaning suggests "a going away."

DECLARATIVE SENTENCES

The cat drank my milk.

Emily was pretty but wicked.

Use a period at the end of a declarative sentence.

IMPERATIVE SENTENCES

Please put the groceries away.

Hand me the pliers.

Use a period at the end of a mild command.

SENTENCES WITH AN INDIRECT QUESTION

Mom asked me which one was my glass.

Andrew wanted to know why he couldn't go to the game with us.

Use a period at the end of an indirect question.

SPACES AFTER THE PERIOD

When typing research papers or essays, place two spaces after the period. Use one space after the period when preparing a manuscript for a printer.

ABBREVIATIONS

Dr. Gregory will be five minutes late.

We live at 306 Minter *St., Ft.* Wayne, Indiana.

The baby weighed exactly 6 *lbs.* at birth.

Use a period to mark the end of some abbreviations. **See also the Abbreviations Chart in the Appendix.**

VERTICAL LISTS

The guest speakers will cover three topics.

1. The German Shepherd
2. The Collie
3. The Australian Shepherd

Use a period after numbers or letters in a vertical list. This includes outlines.

DIALOGUE

Katie commented, "I think those roses are some of the nicest that I've seen."

When writing dialogue, place the period inside the quotation marks.

COMMON MISTAKES

DIALOGUE

Incorrect

Dad asked, "Where's the fire?".

"It is time to go." Sally stated.

She pointed to the painting and said modestly, "I painted that".

Correct

Dad asked, "Where's the fire?"

"It is time to go," Sally stated.

She pointed to the painting and said modestly, "I painted that."

Do not use a period at the end of dialogue that asks a question. Do not put a period at the end of dialogue in the middle of the sentence. Do not place the period outside of the quotation marks.

COMMON MISTAKES

SENTENCES

Incorrect

The cat. Drank my milk.

Correct

The cat drank my milk.

A common mistake with periods is to break up a sentence by inserting a period in the middle.

Note: Except for titles, you should avoid the use of abbreviations in formal writing.

THE
QUESTION
MARK

?

The Question Mark: A punctuation mark put at the end of a word, phrase, or sentence that asks a question.

Etymology: From Anglo-French, Old French, and Latin roots. Its original meaning suggests "to seek."

WORDS

What?

Pardon?

Use a question mark after a word used to ask a question.

QUESTION TAG

This is good, *isn't it?*

I have often wondered why an avocado tree needs a mate close by to produce but orange trees don't, *haven't you?*

Use a question mark after a question tag.

INTERROGATIVE SENTENCE

How far is it to the grocery store?

Will you be coming to the party on Friday?

When is the last day to register for the fall classes?

Use a question mark at the end of a sentence that asks a question (interrogative sentence).

DIALOGUE

"When will daddy be home?" Juliana asked her mother.

"Pretty soon," her mother replied. "Why do you ask?"

When writing dialogue, place the question mark inside the quotation marks. **See also *Quotations.***

QUOTATIONS

AND

QUOTATION

MARKS

" "   **' '**

**Double
Quotation
Marks**   **Single
Quotation
Marks**

Quotations: The punctuation marks used to show the beginning and end of quoted speech or written works.

Etymology: From Middle English where its original meaning suggests "to mark in the margin," and from Latin roots where its original meaning suggests "to number sequentially."

DIALOGUE

When the storm broke the window, my brother shouted, "What is that?"

· Use double quotation marks at the beginning and end of quoted speech.

"It's broken glass!" I responded as I grabbed his shirt sleeve and pulled him away.

Begin a new paragraph whenever you change speakers.

"Quick!" I said, "We've got to get someplace safe."

"Let's go to the basement," he said, "we'll be safe Begin your character's speech with a capital letter, unless it is a sentence interrupted by an identifying tag (who said it). When the identifying tag interrupts the quote, use double quotation marks to enclose each part of the quoted speech. Please notice that the comma after *basement* comes inside the double quotation marks. **See also *Comma.***

Place punctuation marks for your speakers inside the quotation marks.

MULTIPLE PARAGRAPHS

Lord Seymour looked to the eleven lords around the table and said, "Thank you, my honored peers, for coming to this meeting. It has been called to discuss issues of utmost importance.

"We are only a short time away from our landing on this new planet, which has recently come out of an ice age. There are still many areas covered in water. To make our chosen bases habitable, we will begin with land and water engineering operations.

"For these reasons, the initial landing party will be led by my son, Edward. His engineering skills are of utmost importance to our success. He and his crew will begin water and land engineering operations and build our houses and cities."

Lord Seymour bowed his head, ending the formal speech in the custom of their people.

Do not put quotes at the end of a paragraph when the quoted speaker has not changed. Do put them at the beginning of each new paragraph to show that the speaker is still speaking.

INDIRECT SPEECH

Aunt Sue said *that* the kids could come over for the weekend.

Harold suggested *that* everyone meet at the library.

After we told Elvira not to go to the cemetery anymore, she merely responded with a blank stare. Later she told Uncle Art *that* she thought we were all treating her as if she were a child.

Do not use quotation marks when you are referring to what the person said indirectly.

THOUGHT

"I don't care if I hurt his feelings!" Kerensa thought, "Besides, he deserved it!"

Quotation marks can be used to show a speaker's thoughts.

Kerensa thought that perhaps she had hurt his feelings, but then she realized that she was angry enough not to care.

Do not use quotation marks with indirect thoughts.

DEFINITIONS

In English, *grammar* is "the study of how words are put together to make sentences."

Use double quotation marks to define words.

FAMILIAR SAYINGS

"An apple a day keeps the doctor away" is a good motto for modern teenagers.

"Treat others the way you wish to be treated" is sound advice for anyone.

Use double quotation marks to enclose familiar sayings.

WITH COLONS

Thomas writes this: "The earth today shows much man-made damage."

Use a colon to introduce quoted writing. **See also *Colon.***

The new ruling allows "Native Americans to wear traditional dress to graduation": They must also wear a robe over it.

When you use a colon at the end of the quote put it outside of the quotation marks.

WITH COMMAS

"This sure is good catfish," Uncle Pat said, smacking his lips.

While smacking his lips, Uncle Pat said, "This sure is good catfish."

Use a comma to mark the end of quoted speech when the identifying tag (who said it) comes after it. You would not use a comma if the quoted speech is a question or exclamation, or if the identifying tag comes before the quoted speech.

"I think," Johnnie said, "this is a great picnic."

Use a pair of commas when the identifying tag (who said it) interrupts the quote. Please notice that the first comma comes inside the quotation marks and the second comma comes after the final word of the identifying tag. **See also** *Comma.*

Uncle Frank said, "Pass me the potatoes."

Use a comma to introduce the quoted speech when the identifying tag (who said it) comes before it.

WITH SEMICOLONS

The boss said, "I don't want any more lateness"; then he left.

When you use a semicolon at the end of a quote put it outside of the quotation marks. **See also *Semicolon.***

WITH PERIODS

Matilda said, "This is my house."

Put the period inside the quotation marks when the quoted speech comes at the end of the sentence. **See also *Period.***

WITH QUESTION MARKS

Tran asked, "How do I get to the university?"

"How do I get to the university?" Tran asked.

Put the question mark inside the quotation marks. You do not need any other punctuation outside the quotation marks. **See also *Question Marks.***

WITH EXCLAMATION POINTS

When she touched the hot stove, Sally yelled, "Ouch!"

"Ouch!" Sally yelled when she touched the hot stove.

Put the exclamation point inside the quotation marks. You do not need any punctuation outside the quotation marks. **See also** *Exclamation Point.*

SPECIAL USES OF WORDS

The word "indecency" has new meaning in the year 2000.

Use double quotation marks to mark a word when you suggest additional meaning to it or you use it in some other way than is expected. Using double quotation marks to mark a word for emphasis confuses the reader.

Aunt Maude makes a "good meat loaf."

The quotation marks suggest that the meatloaf is not really very good.

QUOTING LONG PASSAGES

Columbus was struck by the beauty and innocence of the Taino people:

> They were very well formed, with handsome bodies and good faces. Their hair coarse—almost like the tail of a horse—and short. . . . They do not carry arms nor are they acquainted with them, because I showed them swords and they took them by the edge and through ignorance cut themselves.

When you quote more than four lines of prose, use indentation instead of quotation marks.

Introduce the quote with a colon, double-space the quote itself, and indent it ten spaces from the left margin.

Most word processing programs allow you to format the entire quoted text with the indentation preset.

TITLES

"The Speckled Band" is my favorite Sherlock Holmes mystery.

Joan Baez sang "We Shall Overcome" at the end of the concert.

"Mayor Cuts Ribbon for New Bridge" is the front-page article.

Use double quotation marks to enclose the title of a short story, newspaper article or column, essay, short poem, song, speech, sermon, pamphlets, or chapter in a book. **See also the entry for** *Titles* **under** *Italics.*

WORDS, PHRASES, AND SHORT PASSAGES OF PROSE

Her favorite expression is "whatever."

My brother's favorite question is "what is that?"

Here the quoted speech comes within the sentence structure itself. Place double quotation marks around the quoted speech. Please notice that *whatever* and *what* do not begin with capital letters because they do not begin a new sentence. **See also** *Capitalization.*

POETRY

Shakespeare writes this about lovers: "How silver-sweet sound lovers' tongues by / Like softest music attending ears."

When you quote only a few lines of poetry, put a slash between each line and use quotation marks.

In "Who Is Tough" Grammie has this to say about today's kids:

> Sometimes I think my kids are rough
>
> And inclined to be a little tough
>
> But then I think of when I was a kid
>
> And of the things I really did
>
> They can't hold a candle by me
>
> And I am glad they did not see
>
> Me and my buddy Jim

When quoting more than three lines of poetry, double-space them and indent each line ten spaces from the left margin. You can preset the margin in most word processing programs.

SINGLE QUOTATION MARKS

Professor Gray Eagle asked, "Where does Columbus refer to the indigenous people as 'handsome' and how did he describe them?"

"What did she say?" Annie asked Hank.

"She said, 'you are late.'" Hank answered as he sat down.

Use single quotation marks to describe a quote within a quote.

THE
SEMICOLON

;

Semicolon: A punctuation mark used in specific instances as an alternative for a comma or period.

Etymology: (Semi-) From Latin roots. Its original meaning suggests "half."

MAIN CLAUSES

In the winter, we usually go skiing; when summer comes, we head for the beach.

David loves to dance; he loves to sing.

You can use a semicolon to join two main clauses when they are closely related in meaning.

MAIN CLAUSES WITH A CONJUNCTIVE ADVERB

The City Council vetoed a road through the Petroglyph National Monument; *nevertheless,* the developer continues to try and change the vote.

The class voted to go to a theme park at the end of the year; some parents, *however,* aren't in support of that.

You use a semicolon to join two main clauses even when the second clause contains a conjunctive adverb like *nevertheless, however, therefore, besides, furthermore, moreover, in addition, likewise, instead, on the other hand, consequently, hence, thus, thereby, for example, then,* and *meanwhile.* Please notice the use of commas with conjunctive adverbs. **See also *Commas.***

CONJUNCTIONS AND MAIN CLAUSES

Laughing loudly, Ramon began to dance; and the crowd applauded enthusiastically.

A little brook, sparkling and clear, ran alongside the trail; and, on the other side, a sheer cliff loomed five stories above us.

Here there are two main clauses linked by a conjunction. Ordinarily, you would use a comma between them. Because each clause contains phrases with commas, use a semicolon to make your meaning more clear.

LISTS CONTAINING COMMAS

We have four new members: Clara from Barelas, Arizona; Marina from Taos, New Mexico; Raquel from El Centro, California; and Betty from Lubbock, Texas.

He has exams on these dates: Friday, September 29, 2000; Thursday, October 26, 2000; Wednesday, December 6, 2000; and Tuesday, January 16, 2001.

When you have a list containing commas, use semicolons between each item in the list.

THE SLASH (VIRGULE)

/

The Slash/Virgule: A punctuation mark used to show a choice.

Etymology: From Latin roots. Its original meaning suggests "a twig or rod."

Alternate Words

Each student needs to bring his/her own lunch.

We could have peas and/or carrots with the roast.

Use a slash between alternate words. There is no space before or after the slash.

Fractions

You need 2 1/2 cups of flour in this recipe.

7/8   15/16   2/3   23/25

A slash is also used to make a fraction. In math books it is also called a *fraction bar.*

Internet

http://www.mtgpublishing.com/index

Slashes are commonly used with Internet addresses, however they have no grammatical meaning. They only help route the computer user to his/her destination.

POETRY

> Estelle Szegedin in her poem "Rejoice" writes: "Do not grieve, rejoice instead / Do not think of me as being dead."

Use a slash to mark the end of lines of poetry when you include it in a quote. Leave a space before and after the slash. **See also** *Quotations.*

THE UNDERLINE (UNDERSCORE)

<u>Underline</u>

The Underline: A line drawn under a word, passage, or title.

Etymology: From Old English roots. Its original meaning suggests "to lie under."

TITLES

My favorite book is <u>Gone with the Wind</u>.

<u>Sesame Street</u> introduced millions of children to reading.

On Saturday, we went to see <u>Abbot and Costello Meet the Mummy</u>.

Underline the title of any major literary work, including television programs, movies, plays, symphonies, operas, books, magazines, newspapers, periodicals, albums, and compact discs. Generally, you use quotation marks to indicate smaller pieces contained within a major work, such as a magazine article, single poem, short story, fable, or essay from a published collection.

TERMS

<u>Grammar</u> is "the study of how words make sentences."

A personal fitness trainer must understand <u>kinesiology</u>.

Underlining a term when you introduce it in a piece of writing. After that, do not underline it again.

Notes:

Underlining and italicizing follow the same rules.

Most word processing programs now allow you to use the Italics feature.

If you are handwriting or using a typewriter then you will need to underline.

SECTION II

STYLISTIC CONVENTIONS

Style: A manner, method, or way of speaking or writing.

Etymology: From Old French and Latin roots. Its original meaning refers to the stylus, an early tool for writing.

TERMINOLOGY

COHERENCE

Coherence is how you use words to tie your ideas together. One way to do this is by using words and sentences that make a transition from one idea to another. These transitions link ideas and show their relationships to each other. **See the Transition Chart in the Appendix.**

DICTION

Diction is how you choose words to create understanding. You need to match your vocabulary to your writing task. In the appendix, look at the vocabulary in the friendly letter. Now look at the vocabulary in the business letter. You will notice that there is a difference. Now, look at the vocabulary in the essay and research paper samples. Choose words and wording to match what you are doing.

PARAGRAPHING

Modern readers have grown to expect short passages called paragraphs. Organizing your texts into paragraphs increases the reader's understanding. Research says that the average paragraph consists of five sentences.

While many texts and teachers have stressed the use of *topic sentences*, a survey of published writers discovered that many do not use them.

Generally, you begin a new paragraph when you move to another topic or sub-topic in your discussion. You can change emphasis in a paragraph by making your point at the beginning of the paragraph or by making your point at the end. Arranging your sentences in different ways can help create the emphasis that you want.

There are also different styles for paragraphs. The two most common are double spacing between the paragraphs or indenting the first line of each new paragraph.

STYLE

Style can be further defined as how you put words and sentences together to express your ideas.

SUGGESTIONS
AND
REFERENCES

SUGGESTIONS FOR CLEARLY EXPRESSING YOUR IDEAS

Original	Improved
During our trip to Denver, *we visited* the zoo, and *we visited* the museum.	During our trip to Denver, *we visited* the zoo and the museum.

State your idea as simply as possible by avoiding unnecessary repetition of words.

She was charged with five *illegal crimes*.	She was charged with five *crimes*.

Avoid using two words that mean the same thing.

There are many girls who want to play soccer.	Many girls want to play soccer.

State your ideas as directly as possible.

The *reason* for his *decision* to visit *Mexico City* was his *desire* to see the *pyramids*.	He visited *Mexico City* to see the *pyramids*.

Whenever possible, reduce the number of nouns so that you can express your ideas simply and more dynamically.

SUGGESTIONS FOR CLEARLY EXPRESSING YOUR IDEAS

Original	Improved
Students *who are on the drill team* have to practice four times a week.	Students on the drill team have to practice four times a week.
Reduce the number of adjective clauses wherever possible.	
The senator is the leader *of ability and honesty.*	The senator is an *able* and *honest* leader.
Dad answered him *in an angry way.*	Dad answered him *angrily.*
Replace prepositional phrases with adjectives or adverbs.	
"Beowulf" is considered *to be* the finest example of Old English poetry.	"Beowulf" is considered the finest example of Old English poetry.
Rewrite sentences to eliminate *to be.*	
The fact that the president appeared on stage nearly caused a riot.	When the president appeared on stage, it nearly caused a riot.
Rewrite sentences to eliminate *the fact that.*	

STYLE SHEETS AND MANUALS

Style sheets and manuals give you all the rules for writing, including punctuation. There are many style sheets and manuals available. Three of the most common are *The Chicago Manual of Style*, *The MLA (Modern Language Association) Handbook for Writers of Research Papers* and the *Publication Manual of the American Psychological Association.*

Many publishers ask for manuscripts following the guidelines of *The Chicago Manual of Style*. You can use the *MLA Handbook for Writers of Research Papers* for English and Humanities topics. You can use the *Publication Manual of the American Psychological Association* for educational, psychological, and social science topics.

Check with your teacher or publisher about what style manual or sheet to use.

OTHER STYLE MANUALS

Biology

Council of Biology Editors, Scientific Style and Format. *The CBE Manual for Authors, Editors, and Publishers,* 6th ed. New York: Cambridge, UP, 1994.

Chemistry

Dodd, Janet., ed. *The ACS Style Guide: A Manual for Authors and Editors.* Washington: American Chemical Society, 1986.

Geology

Bates, Robert L., Rex Buchannan, and Marla Adkins-Heljeson, eds. *Geowriting: A Guide to Writing, Editing, and printing in Earth Science.* 5th ed. Alexandria: American Geological Institute, 1992.

History

The Chicago Manual of Style 14th ed. Chicago: University of Chicago Press, 1993

Journalism

Goldstein, Norm, ed. *Associated Press Stylebook and Libel Manual.* 32nd ed. New York: Associated Press, 1997.

Law
Columbia Law Review. *A Uniform System of Citation.* 16th ed. Cambridge: Harvard Law Review Association, 1996.

Linguistics
Linguistic Society of America. "LSA Style Sheet." Published annually in the December issue of the *LSA Bulletin.*

Mathematics
American Mathematical Society. *The AMS Author Handbook: General Instructions for* Preparing Manuscripts. Providence: AMS, 1994.

Medicine
Iverson, Cheryl. Et al. *American Medical Association Manual of Style.* 8th ed. Baltimore: Williams and Wilkins, 1989.

Music
Holoman, D. Kern, ed. *Writing about Music: A Style Sheet from the Editors of 19th-Century Music.* Berkeley: University of California Press, 1988.

Physics
American Institute of Physics. *Style Manual: Instructions to Authors and Volume Editors for the Preparation of AIP Book Manuscripts.* 5th ed. New York: AIP, 1995

Political Science

American Political Science Association. *Style Manual for Political Science.* Revised ed. Washington: American Political Science Association, 1993.

Science and Technical Writing

American National Standard for the Preparation of Scientific Papers for Written or Oral Presentation. New York: American National Standards Institute, 1979.

Social Work

National Association of Social Workers. *Writing for NASW.* 2nd. Ed. Silver Springs: National Association of Social Workers, 1994.

SAMPLES

FRIENDLY LETTER

525 Mozart Avenue
Alma, TX 57532
May 5, 2000

Dear Uncle Jack,

    Hello, how are you? I am doing really well. I am getting ready to graduate from high school. In the fall I will be attending college. I am very excited. Over the summer, I will be working as a bus boy at a local restaurant. I hope to be able to buy a car.

    What have you been up to lately? Are you still teaching high school math? I'm not very good at math. It's too bad you don't live closer. Then I could get some help with my math courses.

    I have started doing some weight training too. I thought that I might look good with some muscles. Are you still going to become a personal fitness trainer? Are you still coaching?

    I need to go now. I hope to hear from you soon.

                        Sincerely,

                        Your nephew Brad

BUSINESS LETTER

525 Mozart Avenue
Alma, TX 57532

May 5, 2000

Customer Service
Jinkola Company
PO Box 23345
Turkey Junction, AL 62378

Dear Sir/Madam:

On April 23, 2000, I received one of your number 5 soccer balls. I took it to soccer practice where we used it for drills. We practiced for an hour doing dribbling. After that, I noticed that one of the seams had ripped.

I am returning the ball for a refund.

Thank you for your consideration to this matter.

Sincerely,
(four lines for signature)

Brad Gramsky

RÉSUMÉ

Brad Gramsky
525 Mozart Avenue
Alma, TX 57532
(806) 444-7809

Job Objective   Graphic Design

Education   College Preparation
Alma High School
June 1, 2000

**Work
Experience**   2000 to present
Busboy, Taco Bob's, Alma, TX

1998 – 2000
Paperboy,
Alma Herald, Alma, TX

1994 –1998
Yard work, Alma, TX

**Extracurricular
Activities**

Alma Soccer Team

Awards   National Honor Society
Valedictorian

Purpose of an Essay

The purpose of an essay is to "expose a topic" through the use of examples, personal anecdotes, statistics, or other kinds of evidence. It generally expresses the personal views of the author. An essay can be any length. It contains a claim or thesis statement. The remainder of the essay then presents evidence to support the claim. The basic form of an essay is introduction with the claim, body with the evidence, and conclusion.

Short Essay

The thesis statement or claim has been italicized, and the conclusion has been underlined.

To me, skateboarding is much more than a physical activity or sport; to me, skateboarding is a kind of therapy. Whenever I have a bad day, I will go out skating to work out all my anger and aggression by replacing it with the satisfaction of pulling off a difficult trick or maybe learning a new trick. If I ever feel depressed or put upon, I will skate until I am covered in sweat and can hardly even walk back to my house or car and I am definitely not feeling depressed. Loneliness is driven away by the camaraderie that develops when I skate with friends; lack of confidence and shyness disappear revealing a will to do good in all of my endeavors. <u>Consequently, skateboarding is all the therapy that I will ever need.</u>

PURPOSE OF A RESEARCH PAPER

A research paper is a paper of some length based upon either experimental or library research. If your purpose is simply to report, then you write a report research paper. If your purpose is to support a claim, then you must include a thesis statement or claim.

The organization of a research paper is essentially the same as that for an essay. You need an introduction, body, and conclusion. Of course, all of these sections will be longer than those in a short essay.

One of the biggest mistakes made by inexperienced writers is to forget their citations. You must give the source for any ideas that you have quoted, paraphrased, or summarized from someone else.

See the samples beginning on the next page.

RESEARCH PAPER: SAMPLE I

This excerpt from "Navajos and Whole Language: Some Student Success Stories" uses APA style citations.

Vygotsky (1962) accurately notes that when an adult encounters any new problem, he/she goes through the same stages of concept formation as a child. Our two-semester sequence proved adequate for some students but not all. This follows Vygotsky's observations that development is neither linear nor predictable (1962). This suggests that perhaps some approach, which allows students to stay continuously enrolled until meeting exiting criteria should be employed.

Several other notions played an important part in the success of students. Vygotsky (1962) states that a student only learns what he/she finds useful. Kluckhorn and Leighton (1974) make a similar observation about Navajos. In order to bring about maximum learning, then, students must be able to see some application to their own lives before they will learn. Thus, a student cannot use what he/she does not understand (Hubbard 1972) nor learn without stimulating development.

Finally, in order for a student to develop new concepts, instruction must be above what he/she already knows (Vygotsky 1962, 1978).

George Ann Gregory, Ph.D.

unpublished paper

Consult the *Publication Manual of the American Psychological Association*, 4th ed., for more detailed information on citations.

RESEARCH PAPER: SAMPLE I SOURCES

Each research paper must have a list of all sources used for developing it. This comes at the end of the paper.

APA Style Source List

References

Brodkey, D. & Young, R. (1981). Composition correctness scores. *TESOL Quarterly, 15, 2,* pp. 159–167.

Luria, A. R. (1976). *Cognitive development: Its cultural and social foundations.* (Martin Lopez-Morillas & Lynn Solvlaroff translators and Michael Cole editor). Cambridge, MA: Harvard University Press.

Tannen, D. (1985). Relative focus on involvement in oral and written discourse. In David R. Olson, Nancy Torrance & Angela Hildgard (Eds.), *Literacy, language, and learning* (pp. 124 –147). Cambridge: Cambridge University Press.

RESEARCH PAPER: SAMPLE II

This excerpt from "A Comparison of Tolkien's Trilogy and Arthurian Legends" uses MLA style citations.

Gandalf is the wizard in the *Trilogy*. My favorite magic trick that Gandalf does is in the first book when Bilbo has his going-away party. Gandalf made fireworks, and one of the fireworks that he made had a dragon that flew around Bilbo's head.

> It shaped itself like a mountain seen in the distance and began to glow at the summit. It sprouted green and scarlet flames. Out flew a red-golden dragon—not life-size but terribly life-like...(Tolkien 52).

Gandalf also has a sword called Glamdring that is an elfin blade made for the orc wars; the Orcs know it as Foe-hammer. Because it is made for the Orc Wars, it glows with a bluish sheen whenever an Orc is around.

Merlin is the wizard in the Arthurian legends. He sees the future as in the story "Balin and Balan": "...what I behold now fills my heart with grief. But what is to be will be..." (Riordan 10). In addition to being able to see into the future, Merlin is a very great magician. In the story "Excaliber," he puts Sir Pellinor into a deep sleep.

> "Alas," said Arthur as they went along, " you have killed that valiant knight by your magic. Gladly would I have surrendered my life and kingdom rather than to have won the battle thus."

Merlin reassures Arthur that Sir Pellinor is all right.

James Smiley, 6th Grade

For more information, see the **Style Sheets and Manuals** in this section. Also, consult the *MLA Handbook for Writers of Research Papers.*

RESEARCH PAPER: SAMPLE II SOURCES

Each research paper must have a list of all sources used for developing it. This comes at the end of the paper.

MLA Style Source List

Works Cited

Foster, Robert. *A Guide to Middle Earth*. New York: Ballantine Books, 1974.

Lanier, Sidney, ed. *The Boy's King Arthur*. New York: Charles Scriber's Sons, 1945.

Riordan, James. *Tales of King Arthur*. Chicago: Rand McNally and Company, 1982.

Tolkien, J.R.R. *The Fellowship of the Ring*. New York: Ballantine Books, 1976.

APPENDIX

COMMON ABBREVIATIONS

UNITED STATES AND POSSESSIONS

AL	Alabama	**AK**	Alaska
AZ	Arizona	**AR**	Arkansas
AS	American Samoa	**CA**	California
CO	Colorado	**CT**	Connecticut
DE	Delaware	**DC**	District of Columbia
FL	Florida	**GA**	Georgia
GU	Guam	**HI**	Hawaii
ID	Idaho	**IL**	Illinois
IN	Indiana	**IA**	Iowa
KS	Kansas	**KY**	Kentucky
LA	Louisiana	**ME**	Maine
MD	Maryland	**MA**	Massachusetts
MI	Michigan	**MS**	Mississippi
MO	Missouri	**MT**	Montana
NE	Nebraska	**NV**	Nevada
NH	New Hampshire	**NJ**	New Jersey
NM	New Mexico	**NY**	New York
NC	North Carolina	**ND**	North Dakota
OH	Ohio	**OK**	Oklahoma
OR	Oregon	**PA**	Pennsylvania
PR	Puerto Rico	**RI**	Rhode Island
SC	South Carolina	**SD**	South Dakota
TN	Tennessee	**TX**	Texas
UT	Utah	**VT**	Vermont
VA	Virginia	**VI**	Virgin Islands
WA	Washington	**WV**	West Virginia
WI	Wisconsin	**WY**	Wyoming

CANADIAN PROVINCES

AB	Alberta	**BC**	British Columbia
MB	Manitoba	**NB**	New Brunswick
NF	Newfoundland	**NT**	Northwest Territories
NS	Nova Scotia	**NU**	Nunavut
ON	Ontario	**PE**	Prince Edward Island
QC	Quebec	**SK**	Saskatchewan
YT	Yukon Territory		

DAYS

Mon.	Monday
Tues.	Tuesday
Wed.	Wednesday
Thurs.	Thursday
Fri.	Friday
Sat.	Saturday
Sun.	Sunday

MONTHS

Jan.	January
Feb.	February
Mar.	March
Apr.	April
Aug.	August
Sept.	September
Oct.	October
Nov.	November
Dec.	December

ADDRESSES

Ave.	Avenue
Blvd.	Boulevard
Cir.	Circle
Dr.	Drive
Hwy.	Highway
Ln.	Lane
Pkwy.	Parkway
Rd.	Road
Rte.	Route
St.	Street

TITLES

Dr.	Doctor (medicine, chiropractic, doctorate, etc.)
Mr.	A man's generic title
Mrs.	Married woman's title
Ms.	A woman's generic title
Prof.	Professor
Rev.	Reverend (minister)

MEASUREMENTS

in.	inch(s)	**ft.**	foot/feet
yd.	yard	**mi.**	mile
mm	millimeter	**cm**	centimeter
m	meter	**km**	kilometer
oz.	ounce(s)	**lb.**	pound
		lbs.	pounds
teasp.	teaspoon	**tbs.**	tablespoon
c.	cup	**pt.**	pint
qt.	quart	**gal.**	gallon
ml	milliliter	**l**	liter

COMMON CONTRACTIONS

CONTRACTION	WHAT IT STANDS FOR
aren't	are not
can't	cannot
couldn't	could not
could've	could have
doesn't	does not
don't	do not
haven't	have not
he'd	he had/he would
he'll	he will
he's	he is
I'd	I had/I would
I'll	I will
I'm	I am
I've	I have
isn't	is not
it's	it is
she'd	she had/she would
she'll	she will
she's	she is
should've	should have

CONTRACTION	WHAT IT STANDS FOR
that's	that is
there's	there is
they'd	they had/they would
they'll	they will
they're	they are
'til	until
wasn't	was not
we're	we are
weren't	were not
who's	who is
won't	will not
would've	would have
you'd	you had/you would
you're	you are
you've	you have

COMMON HYPHENATED WORDS

All the words included here have separate entries in a dictionary. Many have non-hyphenated counterparts which are a different part of speech or have a different meaning. Spellchecker programs on computers cannot distinguish for you. For accuracy, always check a dictionary.

absent-minded	air-condition
air-cool	air-mail
all-right	all-round
Anglo-American	Anglo-Saxon
baby's-breath	black-eye pea
black-eyed Susan	black-market
black-tailed deer	bold-faced
bow-wow	bread-and-butter
broad-leaf	bye-bye
close-mouthed	corn-colored
court-martial	cream-colored
double-barrel	double-decker
double-edged	double-faced
double-header	double-jointed
double-park	double-quick

double-time
drop-kick

down-to-earth
dry-eyed

false-hearted
fifty-fifty
first-rate
flat-footed
four-leaf clover
free-for-all
full-blooded
full-bodied
full-length

fancy-free
fine-cut
flare-up
fly-by-night
four-wheel
free-spoken
full-blown
full-fledged
full-mouthed

gilt-edged
give-away
good-bye
good-humored
good-natured
good-tempered

give-and-take
gold-filled
good-for-nothing
good-looking
good-sized
goody-goody

hair-raiser
half-blooded
half-life
half-moon
half-tone
hand-knit
hand-to-hand
hard-bitten

half-baked
half-hour
half-mast
half-slip
half-truth
hand-off
hand-to-mouth
hard-fisted

heart-stricken	heart-struck
heart-to-heart	heavy-handed
heel-and-toe	he-man
hide-and-seek	high-class
high-flown	high-grade
high-minded	high-pitched
high-pressure	high-rise
high-spirited	hook-and-ladder
in-between	in-group
knock-knee	know-how
know-it-all	know-nothing
lady-killer	land-grant
lend-lease	life-size
light-fingered	light-footed
lighter-than-air	like-minded
lip-read	long-drawn
long-lived	long-playing
long-term	long-winded
loose-jointed	
make-believe	make-work
man-of-war	merry-go-round

milk-livered

mill-run

north-northeast

north-northwest

open-air

open-and-shut

open-end

open-ended

open-eyed

open-heart

open-minded

open-mouthed

out-of-date

out-of-doors

out-of-the-way

penny-wise

pent-up

pepper-and-salt

pick-me-up

pip-squeak

play-by-play

pow-wow

pull-on

put-put

put-up

rag-a-muffin

red-eye

red-handed

red-hot

right-hand

right-handed

right-minded

salt-and-pepper

sand-cast

saw-toothed

self-appointed

self-assertion

self-command

self-confessed

self-confidence

self-conscious

self-control

self-deception

self-defense

self-denial

self-determination

self-discipline

self-educated

self-employed

self-evident

self-explanatory	self-importance
self-imposed	self-induced
self-indulgence	self-inflicted
self-knowledge	self-pity
self-reliance	self-reproach
self-respect	self-restraint
self-seeking	self-starter
set-to	short-handed
short-lived	short-tempered
simple-minded	single-handed
single-phase	single-space
skin-deep	slow-motion
so-and-so	soft-spoken
south-southeast	south-southwest
stand-in	stand-offish
stick-in-the-mud	sugar-coated
tailor-made	take-down
take-home	take-in
take-off	take-up
thin-skinned	three-color
three-dimensional	three-fold
three-mile limit	three-piece
three-quarter	three-ring circus
time-out	tom-tom
touch-and-go	touch-me-not
two-base hit	two-by-four
two-dimensional	two-edged
two-faced	two-fisted
two-handed	two-name

two-phase
walk-in
water-cool
weather-bound
well-balanced
well-born
well-disposed
well-fed
well-founded
well-grounded
well-known
well-meaning
well-read
well-thought-of
well-to-do
white-collar
write-off

two-ply
wall-to-wall
water-logged
weather-wise
well-being
well-bred
well-done
well-fixed
well-groomed
well-intentioned
well-mannered
well-meant
well-spoken
well-timed
well-written
worm-eaten
write-up

SENTENCE AND
PARAGRAPH TRANSITIONS

Time	previously, earlier, in the past, before, at present, nowadays, meanwhile, later, in the future, eventually
Addition	furthermore, besides, moreover, in addition
Contrast/Conflict	nevertheless, however, conversely, on the other hand, still, otherwise, in contrast, unfortunately
Cause/Effect	therefore, hence, as a result, consequently, accordingly
Comparison	likewise, similarly
Numerical Order	first, second, third, in the first place, in the second place, in the third place, to begin with, next, finally
Spatial Order	at left, nearby, in the distance, below, above, in back, in front